Heal

Candace Cotton

ISBN: 978-0-578-86078-7

Library of Congress Control Number: 2020914944

Cover illustration by Marissa Caggiano

For more information contact: candicotton@gmail.com

Instagram: turtlebreeze
Twitter: turtlebreezee

A healed heart has no vengeance.

As I release, I rise.
As I *heal*, I grow.
I let go.
Light body.
Light mind.

For Natalia and Nasir

You children are my greatest gift. You are me in ways that I cannot always see in myself. Your joy, creativity, and eagerness to learn and become give me the strength to continue in every way, in every day, in every moment. Everything I do, I do for you—today, tomorrow, and forever. My most successful accomplishment in life is the blessing of the God-given gift of being your mother. I will forever cherish you. I will forever protect you. I will forever love you.

For Bugs, Punkin, Squirt, Hoppy, and Ella

May this journey continue to protect and heal you. Listen to your heart—it's the true essence of your existence. Let it guide you, and with everything you do in this life know that you are always protected and loved.

In memory of my mother

Thank you for being my first teacher and greatest mentor. Thank you for sacrificing your life to give me the best lessons, for protecting me, and for raising me to become my best self through my trauma and pain. Your strength enables me to continue to rise. In heaven, on earth, in spirit, and everywhere that you are, we stay connected through love, blood, and soul. No realm will separate the divine connection of our love.

In memory of my father

You passed away before I could remember you—but in my heart, I have always known you to be close. I wasn't even a toddler yet, and you knew how I would be in this world. The nickname you gave me, "Turtle," is one who brings wisdom, travels light, keeps a slow but steady pace, yet finishes first. It proves that I've always connected with the turtle totem; I've always taken my time when others flew by. I knew my journey would meet me as I discovered my true self. I am you in many ways; I am grateful for that. I've lived my life knowing I've always had an angel guiding and protecting me. Now I understand how fortunate I am. Thank you.

Ancestors

Connecting with you has been the best medicine for my wounds. Let's continue this journey of healing and discovering. Stay close, because one thing I'll never let go of is our connection. You paved the way and laid down the foundation; I'm just waking on it, with gratitude, strength, courage, and wisdom. I am you; you are me. Thank you.

Contents

Introduction

My healing doesn't look like pretty yoga pictures in paradise, with vivid sunsets; spiritual vacations with perfect little hippie friends. My healing is painful; it's lonely, dark, and scary. It's real; it's raw, it's honest, it's me. At this moment, it's all of me. My existence. My moment to shine within. To close out the outside world and tend to my needs, for once. I am the star of my own horror show. I am proud to release my demons. With no judgments, no distractions. No one to compare myself to. Nothing to wonder or worry about. I'm naked here, in this place of reflection. I bare my all, but I am here. I am still alive. I am still; silence is all I hear. But my silence is loud; it roars. It buzzes. It screams for freedom. Finally, liberated in my own revelations. Finally, remembering what was never lost but forgotten. The anger towards those who lied and betrayed me. I was a victim of the hell I created for myself by trusting the wrong people. The times when my trust in them made me vulnerable, and I finally felt at home. Just for them to mistake my openness for weakness. Advantages were taken, my innocence was lost, yet again—and again and again.

The mountains I climbed, the tears I shed, watered my flowers, and I became one. My eye stayed on the prize. I forgave but never forgot. Finally, I began to walk into my light; I began to walk into my own victory. My success was my healing. Not a friend in sight, not a shoulder to cry on. Not a single soul to encourage me; in solitude is where they found me.

Yet I am reborn. I am not the same person who hid behind my ideas, who was ashamed of my past and fears. I am a new being, shining so brightly. So light, nothing can weigh me down. I released it all. I am fearless. I can manifest anything I desire. I can go anywhere I want. I can do anything anyone else can. I am flying. I am evolving. I am remembering; I am becoming, I am discovering, I am healing.

heal

I'm the paper and the pen.
I dig within,
find myself in sin,
living
no worries,
sad stories.
Listen carefully as I show you my glory.
My pain.
My healing is insane.
Strength is what I've gained,
to make it to another day.
This war within my mind.
Unhealed trauma is a crime—
no justice, no peace,
just let me release
these thoughts in my head
about what so-and-so said.
This energy is not mine.
Today I got the time.
So let me take you there.
This life ain't really fair.
But it's a gift in disguise,
true as eyes never lie.
Trust yourself and your story.
Soon you'll have your glory.

Your story is your poetry.

I knew I had to be strong in this life,
but I didn't know I had to be a warrior.

candace cotton

Unhealed,
Unloved,
Unlearned.

Let me break,
then heal,
so I can be
whole again.

-*Pieces*

I can't help you heal,
but I hope my words inspire you to.

The tales people tell
will cast you to hell
with one love spell.
Confused and broken,
my heart has spoken.

*These are my **lessons.***

Lessons

Parts of our souls
are stuck in childhoods.
we never healed from.

-Roots

I'm trapped in my own existence.
A prisoner of things I never did,
places I never went, people I never saw.
A wounded child who created a safe place away from the humans
hidden deep inside my own sorrow,
but still safe from them—those monsters.
The nerve of them, staring me down with those ugly eyes of theirs,
pretending to be "perfect".
Yet, they didn't know their own judgment was their illness.
Sick in the mind, with no medicine to cure the hate that possessed
them. To think they thought I was ashamed of the things they hated
about me;
I knew, even then, hate comes from within.
I'm hiding from those beasts, not hiding from myself.
But I'm trapped because the world surrounds them.
Some disguise themselves as friends;
they smile with you,
laugh with you,
bring you in close, just to cut your heart with their canines,
sucking you dry like a leech.
So yeah, I'm stuck.
I'd rather be.
At least I'm protected...

Now you want to love me?

I'm so empty on love,

I only have enough
to give myself this time.

In my mind, there's confusion.
The love we had was just an illusion.
I dreamt of you before we met.
Now, I regret
my fantasy was my vanity—
insanity was you and me.
Crazy love.
You make me crazy, love.

Step away while I unlearn you.
Please let go of what you thought you
knew.
I'm just a wanderer passing through.
This is goodbye, but I don't have to tell
you.
Just look in my eyes;
I'm someone you once knew.

-*Past Life*

You had me,
and then somewhere
we got lost.

You hide your pain
behind your money,
but money
doesn't hide the pain
that's still in your heart.

-Mask

I Miss Us

The place I'm at is cold:
blind eyes,
blurry tears.
emptiness.
Good times, please come save me. I miss us.
It all went so fast.
Happiness.
Where I lay down is where I laid my happiness.
It's been a journey.
The pain is what I remember the most.
Abandoned.
It was easier then...
The world was asleep.
We've awakened to an open wound—
no aid to aid us.
Just us, no justice.
The unexpected is amongst us.
Time and age will not miss us.
Who to trust? Who not to trust?
Isolation,
paranoia,
anxiety...
Please prescribe me something.
I'm crushing.
Good times, please come save me.
I miss us.

Now that you're losing, you're humble.
But that's not who you are.
That's just where you are.

My eagerness to feel love again
overlooked the darkness
that surrounded you.

I saw what I wanted;
I felt what I desired.
You emptied your vessel of
insecurity, trauma, and pain
into my heart,
which was filled with love.

In order to get whatever you could
to survive,
no matter the consequence,
self-serve was your agenda.

I was conned by your charm,
your smile,
your potential.

I mistook your jealousy for admiration.
My unhealed spirit attached to yours.

Twin flames, we both showed reflections—similar desires,
different intentions.

I don't have to read your mind
when I can feel your energy.

Does she protect or destroy?
The intent is good but made with distress and ploy.
It does not matter who is offended
as long as her desires are intended.

Plotted and schemed, jealous prune,
delusional fears,
afraid to lose
what was never hers.

Deeply wounded, skin is thick.
Voice is deep.
Does not fear what she should.
Consequences never go unanswered.

Old lady, know better.
Too late for her,
the time has come—
never apologized
for what she's done.

-Out-law

You envy my light
because you fear
your own darkness.

Evil eye and bitter face
hide in snake skin.
Secrets sit within.
Eyes reveal true stories,
shade them with frames.
Corrupted soul looking to blame,
envious of those who love—
dark shadows cover him.

His lies surface; his karma hits.
Million-dollar smile,
charm, and wit,
smooth yet humble—
matches vibes.
Make-believe, trained to pretend.
Real life or on screen,
survival mode by any means,
masked with good intent.
Sees what he wants.
Denial of the truth he shows.

-The Actor

I never want to be anywhere,
ever again, where I am not
loved.

I wanted you to fit
into the picture
I created.
I'm not perfect,
but that picture was.

Confused between your world and mine—who are you?
Who am I when I am with you?

-Lost

Tragic muse you are—
my dark inspiration.
I guess I'm using you just like
you're using me, but that's not
my intention.

You are truly hard to love.

They hurt you.
Then go about their way,
But those scars stay.

I want to heal that part of me
that so desperately needs you.
I don't want to care about
how you move when I'm not
around.

Tonight is especially cold.
I haven't heard from you all week.
I constantly question:
What did I say?
What did I do
to make you disappear into silence?
But I choose not to wallow in my pity;
It's a broken record by now.
The truth is, you're weird.
You've always been weird;
It was a red flag that I overlooked,
because I understand no one is perfect.
Leave people alone though.
Go heal those wounds.
I didn't hurt you, but someone did.
You didn't deserve me, but someone does.
You've left a bad taste in my mouth, but I still have my appetite.
See, I won't punish my future with a bitter past.
And the more I think about it...
I'm glad you left.

-Cold Chicken

Imagine being in love with someone
you don't have to chase.

Was I lost,
or was I buried so deep that I could not see my own eyes?
I could feel,
I could move,
but I could not see
the destruction that was being exposed right in front of me.
I was so lost in you.

You were my bad habits.
You were my distractions.
You were my crutch.
You were everything I needed to avoid the hurt inside of me
because your pleasures
were so much more comforting
than my pain.

Then you became my pain,
which forced me out of my head
and back into myself.
Looking for answers,
looking for purpose,
looking for me—again.

-*Lost You, Found Me*

Cut the cord so I can breathe.
Let me go. I wish to be free
of you, of me, of this, of us.
Tied to the soul, of burdens and lust.
I'm healing, yet you're filling
my soul with toxicity and waste.
Letting go has been my safe place.
Obligations and guilt
form the house that you built.
Release the chains
so I can fly.
I have no regrets
and no goodbyes.

If you can't love me,
don't hurt me.
Just leave me.

The bitterness of a jealous woman bleeds through her soul.
The dark shadows under her eyes can't hide her malicious intention
to ruin anything she feels is better than she.

-Insecure

She hated her mother, her father as well,
relentless and cold, Jezebel from hell.
Abandoned her only son
for cigarettes and rum.
Slouched on the couch,
drunk and high,
eyes to the sky,
hoping to die.
Wakes up
just to cover her scars with makeup.
Always in denial—it's never her fault. Everyone's to blame.
Now her son is ashamed.
Narcissist is his name.
Now he is her. The roles have changed.
Wounded and hurt,
everything stays the same—cursed.

-Generations

You can't give me what you don't have to
give yourself—love.

-Empty

I'm numb—can't breathe anymore.
I'm trying, but what are we fighting for?
Ups and downs are getting too tough.
Can't let go—there's nothing to let go of.
It's not what I want to hear,
but the message is clear.
You love without fear.
I protect 'cause of my past,
afraid we won't last...*So I let go.*

Things I Never Did

I never got married.
Because I never kissed the guy of my dreams.
It all seems like a blur now, and I'm wondering what it really
means... Does it mean anything? Would it change who I am, or
where I am, and what I'd be?
Questions constantly flood my mind.
What if I did what I never did?
Would I be where I want to be?
Or, because the things I never did, is why I'm exactly where I
should be. My perspective is my key,
lower and higher self calling the shots.
I listen to both depending on my mood...
Depending on my patience,
depending on my trauma,
depending on what day it is.
I'm like an unwritten map; Zigzags lead the way, clear my path, and
remove my blockages.
I'm trying to go where I've never been.
I'm trying to do things I never did.
But there is this unhealed hurt sitting
and manifesting in my head—
Telling me, I'm not good enough,
I'll never make it,
and to give up.
My inner child wants to run the show.
I calm her down with temporary joys.
She's good for now until she's triggered again.
Heal, my child. Those ghosts don't exist.
You've grown, but you're not done growing.
I release her and let her be.
We have places to go and
things to do that we never did.

Your eyes are covered in costume,
disguised to hypnotize.
Your intent is unclear.
Confused, conflicted—
something's wrong with this picture.
It's blurry and cracked
already—we just met.
This is a sign.
Let's not waste more time.
I'm just not feeling your vibe.

-Trust Issues

You became the victim of a crime you did to me.
That was your way of survival.
Have the world pity you
with your dramatic details
of all you went through—only, in reality it was you
putting me through trauma
that has become your testimony.

-The Story You Tell

Let me see your bad side so that I can love all parts of you. -

Attemptation

He conveniently stopped talking to me—his convenience.
It reminded me of what pain feels like.
I visualized the breakaway; no explanation,
Just plain ghost, dead silence.
No trigger warning.
I suppose that was his trauma response.
Fear hits, take off—fly away.
It's always easier in the moment to run.
It made me realize more about myself...
How I continued a relationship with the potential of what
I'd fantasize we could be—
Yet, we were too different; It felt forced.
But I couldn't be the one to express that.
I suppose he did, but in a cold way.
I guess it's better now.
We both are free, and the lesson is learned.
Don't stay where you're not loved,
even if you fantasize about what it could be.
I always just pay attention to what it is.

-Flight

Not loving myself

was probably my worst heartbreak.

Don't buy me flowers.
I am the flower.
Don't pick me up.
Let me down.

Let me go.

I know your intentions aren't pure.

Whatever it is that you want,
I don't have it to give.
I see myself years from now,
healing the heart you broke.

I'm doing well without you.

Don't interrupt me.

I told you too much in the beginning.
I became an opportunity for you.
I became a project you worked.
You had numerous angles.
I was blind not to see your true intention.
You hid it in plain sight.
I began to see your deceitful ways with people you loved the most.
I began to see a cycle of generational bitterness that continued to get passed down from one seed to the next.
The people you say you loved were so much like you in so many ways—jealous and unforgiving.
I blocked out the thoughts that did not originate from my soul, the thoughts that take my existence into a tailspin of painful visions that manipulate the present truth.
The theory of fears and scenarios rushes through my head when I refuse to let go of something that kills me every day.

I've been hurt more than I've been loved.

The stillness of the room captured your faux
flowers promptly placed in a basket.
Everything is still.
It doesn't move, yet it moves you.
Its presence stands out—betrayed beauty
deceived by looks, thin to the touch.
Abandoned soul, vessel is present. You're
present—your gift, your reflection. *You.*

-Deception

Did I not come here to be loved?
If not, why is love always the mission? Why is it always the goal?
Love me, look at me! I'm smiling. Look how pretty my teeth
are. See? "Cheese!"
How could you walk away and not acknowledge my greatness?
Now I'm sad; nobody loves me.
Not even me. How could I?
How could I love me when the world hates me?
The world hates what God gave me, so therefore I should.
I should change it to fit what they want to see, not what God
wants me to see.
Isn't this correct?
Isn't this what you created?
The system you built; this is your design.
But you laugh at me because I am different.
Then you laugh at me when I change my differences for *you*—to
be loved, by you.
But what about me?
What about what I want?
What about how I feel?
If God created me in image of himself,
then I am.
If I am me and God is God, then what does that make you?

-Supreme Colors

I wanted us to be over.
Now I just miss the old
days.

Some people never see the bad they do to others

until life shows them.

I don't have to see your eyes, but I feel them on me.
I don't have to know what you're thinking, but your energy
speaks; It tells me your secrets and the things you hide, just like
your eyes. You cover them with glass but you're not invisible; I
see you looking, silently peeking through.
You hide your face, so your intentions aren't showing,
but ghost energy always comes with a motive.
What's your angle? I know you have one...

-Who Sent You?

Your enemy was your friend first.

They never miss a good thing until they
can no longer take it for granted.

There's light inside my heart and
every time it breaks it opens.

-*Duality*

heal

I got away. You lose.

An insecure,
lost man,
poor but with potential.
Morals are absent.
Self is centered.
Soul is empty,
lacks intelligence,
easily influenced,
advantages taken.
Lucky by gifts,
fooled by fantasy—soul is sold.

-Celebrity Slave

Silly girl feels entitled by titles.
Materials cover her pains but don't protect or heal her.
Gains joy through the struggles of others.
Heart is broken but replaced with false images of pretend life,
like a little girl playing in her dollhouse.
Doesn't know reality from childhood.
Unhealed neglect from absent father.
Out for delusional revenge against those she envies.
Afraid they want what kills her.
Afraid to look within to heal broken pieces.
Victim by nature, her soul bleeds from misery.
Can't escape; has nowhere to go.
Lost in someone else's false dream.
Stuck and blocked—that's the life she leads.

-Trophy

How could we have gotten to know each other
when we didn't even know ourselves?

heal

If I could give you my pain for a day so that you could feel me for once,
I still wouldn't.
But I can't continue to convince you it hurts—
where it hurts and why it hurts.
That's pain in itself; that you can't see my struggles.
So, you can't understand my love, or my hate, or my anger, or me.
Will you allow me to teach you?
I tried that.
You called me controlling.
Your mystery is your insecurities.
Your secrets are the lies you tell yourself.
I pray for the day you come clean so that you can heal.
Stop wearing a mask and reveal
your true self.
Maybe then, you will feel my pain.
Because then, you'll see what it's like to truly be free.

So, what's your excuse now?
You'll find one. You always do.
This is who you are.
You've revealed your true self.
I'm still in love with the impressions.
It's my fault though.
I made love to Satan himself.
My choice,
ghost mind,
lustful heart wants what it wants.
Give me a gun with no bullets and
I'll pretend to kill this.
But deep down, I'm hoping you get it right.
Hoping you see all the good in me.
See, this catch is so good, yet you keep missing it.
This ain't meant,
"let it be," you say.
This ain't it.
This ain't real love.
Too much of a fight.
I can struggle alone.
I created you,
not you as in your existence, but you, as what I
imagined you'd be for me. Like in the movies.
Yet you never showed up.
This is how our story ends.
The future me knows it's a happy ending...

I hate resisting the love I still have for people who have hurt me, but today I choose me.

-Self-Love

Sorry if my distance offends you,
but I heal better in solitude.

After you've hurt me,
you don't get to know me ever again.

-Closure

I'm not waiting on anyone to come save me.

The moment I forget
is the day you'll remember.

Find yourself.
Then come find me.

Eventually you'll learn how to save yourself.

I pray
you find someone you can trust.
I pray
your karma humbles you.
You'll learn.
I pray you learn...

-Lessons

I'll plant the seed, but you have to water it.

-*The **Heal**er*

Heal

I lost it all:
friends, lovers, goals. I lost it all and began to remember who I was.
Underneath all the filtered fake energy was this little girl still wiping
her tears from the wounds that never healed.
Pain covered me like makeup;
tears washing me like a rainy day.
I was soaked,
drained,
lost,
hidden,
forgotten,
unloved...
Yet still, this light of hope is what kept me alive.
This isn't all there is...
I constantly questioned myself during my tormented moments of
agony.
It gets better. It has to...

I use to believe the only way I could feel love was to be loved.
I searched and searched but still ended up feeling empty and lost
with even more hurt to heal from."Keep going"! There's this
voice again telling me to keep going, keep shedding, keep
remembering who you are.
Your true self is hidden deep beneath the scars. There you are—
you're *there.*
Keep washing away all the things they taught you to be and
keep remembering who you are destined to be, and once you do,
you'll see that the greatness was already there.
You'll discover yourself,
your talents, your gifts.
You'll discover your happy place.
It will be you, the love of self.

All this time, it was always you that you were looking for.

heal

Things die when you let them go.

-Fall

Justice for the good-hearted.
There's a war on those who love hard.
But good things come to those who heal;
time slows down when you're sad
and when you're hurting.
Take away the present
and take away the past.
Look ahead for the glory
that is owed to you
by the work you do.
Rejection will direct you—
Back to self again.
Then your present
will start to feel like yourself again.

-Home

heal

Wait until you meet the healed you.

I'm patient because love is patient.
I am love.

3:33 a.m.—full moon.
Listen to the sounds of silence.
Feel the touch of loneliness.
Smell the aura of solitude.
Taste the breath of healing.

Loving myself is how I healed
the pain from others
who didn't love me.

I am the gift.
My presence is the present I give myself.

-Gratitude

~~Unhealed,~~

~~Unloved,~~

~~Unlearned.~~

Healing,

Loving,

Learning.

She evolved through her trauma.
Her discomfort healed her.
With only two options—die or survive—
she chose to live.
With every ounce of her love she bared through
the birth of her children, alone and abandoned.
He told her she wasn't getting the fairytale, as he
eloped with his mistress;
full of pride and entitlement,
success and fame, lights and cameras, claimed his
name.
The picture looks perfect from the outside
looking in,
but the truth lies beneath when his story will end.

Broken pieces,
shattered tears,
clear like glass,
cuts like fire,
burns like salt...
Where did I go wrong?
It hurts like hell.
Who gon' save us?
You choose your choice. Stand
away. Leave!
It's best for you;
I'll handle it like I always do.
Strength, call me strong.
Woman.
Yes, a woman.
Womb-man: I create hue-mans.
Listen to me:
Don't fear the unknown. Listen
to me: Don't fear me. Just listen
to me:
I'm not what you think,
I'm not what you've heard. I've
survived, I am surviving. I lived,
I am living.
I healed, I am healing.
Listen to me:
Do not fear growth.
It is the only way out.
Pain is needed, love is needed.
You are needed.
Heal.

A healed heart knows better.

That thing that once gave you butterflies
now annoys and bugs you like flies.
Every day you heal, he fades.
His presence gets lighter, like see-through.
He felt entitled to your heart with his
rejections and your persistence.
You begged and cried for him but were lost and hurt.
He is excused.
This trash stinks; throw it in the can.
This is old news. Now bring me today's paper.

-Detached

heal

She moved on and discovered herself.
Her joys were free of guilt and burden.
Love didn't cost.
She escaped a life she once felt entitled to when she
was lost deep inside someone else's truth.
She was given a new map that she drew out:
no traffic, no lines, her mission, her route.
She wasn't looking for love because she had it inside.
She was looking for life, her tribe, her guides.

Her journey a never-ending story—
but freedom, light, and healing were her glory.

You know you're healing when you no longer look for
things that hurt.

My Dream

I had a dream I survived.
The mood is always shocked,
never really accepting my present fate
always working towards the change.
Justice runs through my veins.
I felt if they were punished, it would free me. I
would smile and say, "See?
You got what you deserved!"
But I knew my healing was my justice,
and their punishment wasn't going to change what
changed me.

I deserved better, and I had to create
a better place,
in my heart;
it had to be quality.
I was an innocent kid
being punished by the cruelty,
but I dreamt I survived,
and that's what kept me alive.
The wrong people appeared
at the wrong time.
I had been there already;
I could see through
their intentions like glass.
Everyone had a motive:
good or bad.
A need to fill a void within themselves.
They looked outside, instead of within themselves.
But in my dream, I survived.

Heal,

so you don't continue to fear
what you've experienced...

heal

I feel more when I let go.
My wounds are open, yet healed energy protects them.

I'm a lighter being with less baggage blocking
the love I've hidden for years.

It's time to live again, love again. Breathe again.

It feels good when you let go...

Kingdom Come

Deep down, I hated him.
But I held my breath and closed the phone.
I'm in this alone, on my own.

Love spells, secret tales,
cries at night, toxic fights.
He's the blood and I'm the bone.
I'm strong like fire; it's my throne.

Yet, I allowed him to make me feel like I wasn't Queen.
Too caught up in this lustful scene.

Cut the cameras; the show is over.
I say goodbye, and that's my closure.

He asked her, "Why are you single?"
She replied, "Because I enjoy myself."

-Healed Energy

candace cotton

If pain brings you wisdom,
imagine what healing will bring.

heal

I heal every time I remember parts of myself
that I thought were lost
forever.

If my silence hurt you while I was healing,
for that I apologize.
But my solitude was what saved me
when no one else was qualified
to be there... Let's be fair:
I shut the door and pushed them away,
too ashamed of my pain.
I didn't want anyone to stay,
looking down on me, as if their lives were so great.
When you heal, you feel everything in every little
way.

Don't Forget

Forget the pain.
Don't forget the lesson.
Don't forget the blessing.
Don't forget the reason.
Don't forget the meaning.
Don't forget the season.
Don't forget the teaching.
Don't forget the struggle.
Don't forget that you're winning.

The healer heals herself.

You deserve the love you
daydream about.

Phoenix

They weren't meant to stay but to teach.
Funny, right?
The ones we wish we never met
become our greatest teachers...

I often reminisced about where I would be
had I not learned those painful lessons that
could have killed me.

It was close, yet I chose life.
I chose to dig myself out
of the grave they buried me in.
I was alive and breathing, but barely.

Giving up was always the easiest thing, but
my story deserved a better ending.

I deserved a better living.

I focused on what I had gained
and erased everything that was lost.

Why swim in my tears
when the sunrise never failed to save me?
Drowning in my pity, I had risen;
I was saved and I was healing.

Getting over someone
without having to get under someone else
is true healing.

You are the plant you need to water and nourish every day.

Never go back to what you've healed from.

Your love is greater than your fear.
Focus on your love.

If you don't heal from your
past, then everyone you
meet will feel like a shadow
of it.

It's dark in here, so shadows follow me.
I'm digging, scratching, screaming:
"Let me out!"
Move out of my way; I'm trying to be freed.
I'm worn...
Look in my eyes, see my tears,
feel my fears.
I breathe in, release, now step away.
I look back at you
and tell you goodbye, forever.
It was a lesson, but now I must move.
I removed you and I moved.
Blood was shed, tears were dropped.
Sweat drips and I drift away
from this scene.
I leave you with the illusion of my presence:
You will never forget me.
Every time you reflect on our magic,
you will block it out with a temporary high.
But I will always stay an image
sitting beneath your eyes.
Tattoo tears.
Cries in the night.
The darkness takes you and fills you with regret.
I wish you well,
but it's my breakthrough. I raise my chin and
look at the sky. Nothing is holding me;
I'm flying. I'm freeing all those demons...
Goodbye!
I smile at you, blow you a kiss, and send you on
your way.
This is it...
Until next lifetime.
This is all I have to give.
Now my new life begins.

New Birth

I'm running out of places to hide—
my distractions, I've become immune.

I'm tired of being on the other side,
but I'm finding myself; I'm in tune.

Light reveals true stories
of dark matters hidden within.

I'm searching for my glory,
and knowledge of self is where it begins.

When you start healing,
you stop hiding.

Crying is a sign of healing,
not a sign of weakness.

The moment you admit you need healing
is the moment your healing begins.

heal

Without self-love—you'll always look for
things outside of yourself to fill you.

Forgive, and then *forget them.*

Your home won't be happy
if you're not happy.
You gotta heal yourself first.

Stay positive,

but still cry if you have to.

People try to break you
because they're broken.

When you're evolving
nobody really knows you—
they knew you.

You gain inner peace
by knowing when to be silent.

The more you heal
the less offended you get.

When you have nothing to hide,
no one
has anything to use against you.
Be free.

Unhealed trauma will create issues in your mind that don't exist,
especially if you've been hurt over and over.
Remind yourself to stop looking for things
that aren't there.

Never feel guilty for protecting
yourself from people who
never felt guilty for hurting
you.

The heart is meant to *break*—that's how it opens.

Inhale. Then exhale pain.

Am use me then park

The icy line between reality and fiction
it's all a fantasy ride I choose to stand in line for.
The thrill feels like magic; I'm high like mountains.
My heart is on fire, but it's that good flame,
that twin flame. That flame that lights an engine
and flies me away on a mental vacation,
where he and I exist as one heart beating so
heavily— I'm touched.

It doesn't matter what the norm is or what anyone
else thinks
because we've finally found each other through
the mist of the darkness
that surrounds the world.

His light and my light equals the sun, and here we
are surrounded as one—
love we've created, and it feels so good.

I live in this moment so innocent and free, not
realizing one day, the ride is over.
And it's not my choice but the choice.
Bittersweet because love has no attachments, but
it's still so sweet that
I'll have that memory, that high, that feeling I'll
hold tight in my heart.
And when I think about him, I'll smile because I
was blessed
to have experienced something so loving. And for
that, I'll always be grateful.

I loved him more than he knew.
If only he knew that I still do...

What triggers you, controls you—heal

As you heal,
everything else around you heals.

Eventually, our pain becomes our blessings—
our dark becomes our light.

Healing is transcending.

You learned the
hard way...
but the point is,
you learned.

If you only knew just how healing self-
love can be, you'd love yourself.

candace cotton

I was lost in this
world but I found
myself.

I am sleep.

Wake me up, and show me a mirror,
and then I will see that I am the creator of all my troubles.
Once I acknowledge that I am the creator of all my pain,
I am then able to fix them by fixing myself.
You see, the only person in my way is me.

It's not me against the world, it's just me against me.

I am the problem. I am the solution.
I am the student. I am *the teacher.*

The Teacher

Relationships are teachers.

heal

In a league of her own,
the only thing she followed
was her truth.

One thing stronger than your pain
is your gift.

Three a.m.—full moon.

They reject you, then belittle you because they know you deserve more than they can ever be. They know you are great and fear your greatness. So they leave you wounded, hurt, and vulnerable for a quick fix. They string you along and feed off that energy, knowing they have no intentions to become what you desire in them. Yet no one else can have you because you becoming who you are truly meant to be will trigger their egos. They get joy out of playing with your heart, and the chase you provide feeds their false sense of worth. They gain delusional power of self off the weakness of the hearts they break. The only power they have is the power you give them.

Remember who you are. Remember who you were before them.

Full moons always feel like the end of a chapter.

Coddled from the Womb

You don't choose us because you never chose yourself.
They are an escape from the reality you face.
You bury your bones to hide your truth,
but soon, the rain pours down
and you become stuck in the mud.

Confused and lost, you continue to hide your identity,
hoping no one sees what lies beneath those brown eyes.
Our image reminds you of that,
so you hate us, belittle us, abuse us—
and you don't protect us.
You prefer that we die so you can continue this facade, but
your disconnection is your own weapon against thyself.

Oppressed by you, we share the same blood,
but we are oppressed *by you.*
See that?
You praise us with your words
and shatter us with your actions.
You're a trend; you blend in.
Physically desired and placed on a pedestal,
given flowers you've never earned.
You have such a delusional sense of entitlement
that your arrogance bleeds through your skin,
sweat dripping off your confused face.
We scream at you to wake up
because we know you can't hear our cries.
Yet you call us emotional and bitter,
angry and undesirable,
fat and ugly—what have you.

But aren't we *you,* an image of *you?*

We are something you chase to erase
until the end of time—
until your time has ended,
and the flowers have died.
The status falls down,
the crowds fade out,
and the curtain closes.

You've sunken your own ship.
Now you're drowning in despair
with one hand out calling for help
from the people you rejected,
belittled, and left for dead.

Now *you're* dead
on the inside
and bitter all over.

We pray for you.
We hope you grow.
We hope you learn.
And most importantly,
we hope you heal, teacher.

Playing the role before it's manifested is also attracting it.

Please stop punishing yourself for the things
you did when you were growing.

Work on being
unoffended by healing the
wounds that trigger you.

Life has been treating you
exactly how you've been treating yourself.

.

Let the light heal you.
Let the light lead you.
Let the light teach you.
Let the light inspire you.
Eventually, you'll become what you engage in the most.
Become the light.

When we understand people better,
we can love them better
because then
we'll understand how they love.

Be loyal to your intuition.

Don't become a vessel full of resentment, anger, and pain because that's all you'll continue to attract.

Let go.

heal

I was left—
Left to pick up the shattered pieces of glass that
broke my heart and cut me to shreds. I bled for
years.
Everything triggered me.
Paranoia haunted me.
I trusted no one…
not even me.

I had to push myself to do things
I thought would bring me light in my dark days,
but they only brought me pain,
storms, and more rain.
So, I told the world goodbye for now;
I had to lose them and lose myself
to find something else—
a place where I was safe
from the evils of the world
that traumatize the good-hearted.
The ones who give and the ones who love, only
to be forgotten, replaced, and erased.

Stillness discovered me.
It told me to listen
to the noise I can't hear,
where there is no fear.

"You lack nothing.
You are everything you are looking for: a teacher
within. You are a treasure: gold bleeds through
your veins. Your smile brightens your darkest
days.
They'll look hard, but they won't find you in
anyone else. Because they took your kindness for
granted,
and they'll miss you,
wishing for that time again,
but the youth that spoke the truth won't allow
that time again.
Now be free! You are released."

I was found...

You really gotta trust the seeds
you're planting will manifest.
If you don't believe in yourself,
the universe won't either.

When you love yourself, you don't require the world to.

The new person you're looking to replace
to fill that void *is you.*

The person talking to me in my dreams is my higher self.
Teaching me unconsciously
what it means to really be free—flying high no worries, just free,
and high—
No worries.

heal

You'll never have to force anything
that's truly meant for you.
When you find yourself
forcing a situation
or going out of your way
to show someone how great you are
—*it's time to walk away.*

Watch how strong you become
when you let go of the things not meant for you.

You deserve better;
and better isn't another person,
better is you.

Don't compare your seeds to other people's crops.
We're all on separate journeys.
They might be winning
because it's their season to bloom.
Be patient.

You get what you give yourself.
You want loyalty? Be loyal to yourself.
You want love? *Love yourself.*

You can't change people,
and you can't wait on people to change.

heal

Gratitude.

Love yourself so that you attract
the people who will love you.

Your manifestations mean nothing
if you don't show gratitude
for what you already have.

Be careful who you allow in your life
when you're hurting.
Vulnerability can open your heart
and mind
to the same toxicity
that you left.

Stay a mystery.
Only the right people are meant to understand you.

Just because you're over something
doesn't mean you're done healing from it.

Your ancestors will keep removing the wrong people—as long as you keep asking for protection.

People's true colors come out
when they don't get
what they want from you.

You might not be where you want to be right now,
but a seed has to grow.

I'm not interested in teaching anyone how to love me anymore.
I'm past that.
I attract what I need now.

-Growth

Heal your pain before trying to replace it.

Not everyone is meant to travel
the road you've been destined to lead.
Free yourself from unwanted baggage.

You don't need to trust people to maneuver in life.
You just need to make sure you trust yourself enough
to choose the right people to maneuver with.

Trust the universe
is going to place you
exactly where you need to be
for that opportunity you've been manifesting.

Cleanse your mind of toxic distractions and evolve from the illusions.
Find your true purpose in life.
Never settle.
Never get too comfortable.
Keep moving.
Keep growing.
Keep evolving.
Change is good.

Embrace the new you when it arrives.

They were the blockage.
They're gone.
Now you're back.

People change,
but when they do,
it won't be for you.

You give people power over you
when you put them on pedestals.

Remember who you are.

heal

Rejection will teach you how to love yourself.

This is a reminder.
Don't go back to what you've healed from.
Familiarity is tempting because it's comfortable,
but nothing grows there.

If you want doors to open,
you gotta remove what's blocking them.

Everything about love should be mutual.

Are bad things happening to you?
Or is life just teaching you?

Sometimes it takes us seeing our flaws
in other people
for us to acknowledge
they exist within ourselves.

The more you love yourself,
the more you'll detach from the things that don't love
you.

The love you give yourself
is how you gain the love from
within.

heal

Teach yourself how to let go,
the same way you teach yourself how to hold on.

People don't deserve all of you; save something.

Whoever is responsible for your happiness
will be responsible for taking it away.

candace cotton

You are the manifestation; all you have to do is speak your intent.

Let go and allow yourself to be loved, beloved.

Kindness is often mistaken for being naïve.
The kind person knows this and acts accordingly.

Your pain is life teaching you.
Your joy is life celebrating you.
You can't have one without the other.

If someone is trying to abandon you, let them.

It will come when you are ready to receive it.

Keep visualizing your comeback.
The universe is listening.

heal

I know you want to teach people how to love you.
But they have to learn how to love themselves first.

Be your authentic self.
That's loyalty to you.

Listen to your heart—it's the true essence of your existence.

Free yourself from the approval of others by not
being consumed by their opinions of you.

The more you heal, the less you need.

The truth should enlighten you, not offend you.

Your twin flame is your higher self.

Endings turn into new beginnings.
Never get too wrapped up in a sad moment.
Life's forever changing.

Live your life free from attachments,
if you have nothing to hold on to.
Then you'll have nothing to let go of.

If it's raining in your life, it means you're growing.

Honesty is quality.

candace cotton

When people are removed,
that's the universe protecting you.

Life is getting harder so that you can get stronger;
understand the evolution of preparation.

Your energy is your
unspoken language.

I promise you—you don't have to hurt others to win in life.

candace cotton

Recharge yourself

by unplugging the distractions.

Can you really love yourself
and hate other people?

Your hardest lessons
usually come from someone
you loved the hardest.

You don't fit in. *Embrace that.*

We made it to the future.

-2020

The origin of a new era has arrived.
A new decade filled with hope, love,
transitions and transformations.
Healing is upon us; stay protected.
Carry yourself with love, walk with
peace—give and give some more.
Living over purpose,
moments over memories.
Present over past.
You made it to the future.
Now, let go.

The world is evolving,
and so should you.

Now is the perfect time
to discover who you really are,
not who they told you to be.

heal

If your happiness
is solely based on
the pleasures
of material possessions,
you will emotionally suffer
trying to constantly maintain it.

Money masks the truth of true intent of survival.
Money has blood on its hands—
the faces of products,
the masters of sin.

heal

The things you're doing without
you didn't need anyway.

candace cotton

If you feel
like you have no way,
that's a sign it's time
to create your own.

Find those people who are like you.
Connect with them, and
build with them.
Grow with them,
and *heal the world with them.*

What's meant for you will find you.

heal

Start reading eyes more.

The new awakening.
As evil dies out,
Light shines on.

heal

Plant your seeds now 'cause we're growing.

candace cotton

The light is exposing true intentions.
Pay attention.

The people who weren't meant for you were removed.
That's a blessing.
Give thanks.

New life energy.
Feel it and allow it to manifest.

Some people don't want the truth
because the lie is so much more comforting.
The truth is here.

It's alive.

Keep taking care of yourself,
and the universe
will take care of you.

heal

Detach and unplug.

Connect back to nature.
Connect back to self.

232

The answers lie within.

Unlearn false teachings,
and discover what's true for you.

You're protected.
Stop worrying.

God energy is all around you.
Tap into that.

You'll never be who
you once were—
that's the point.

candace cotton

I apologize to anyone I hurt
when I was hurting—and
healing myself

-Mommy

Mommy

You never really know
how much you love someone
until it's time
to finally let them go.

Going to sleep was never the same again.
I knew when I had awakened, you'd still be gone.
Every day until the rest of my life, you'll still be gone.
I began to wonder what I did wrong
and what I could have done to make your life better.
I blamed myself because all I've ever
wanted was to help everyone,
but I had to leave in order to do that. I
know you understood my journey.
It's scary now, though—
This new world without
you. I feel alone and I'm missing you.
I'm making the best of my days with the
babies. They're a pair, them two.
It's what I'd imagine and hope you'd see. But I
feel your energy. I know you see.
In another sight. Another way. Another
world. Maybe a bird visiting me,
or your memories in my sleep.
But you, in all the forms of existence, still exist.
I'm thankful for that.
The knowledge I have of myself makes me aware of that;
It's something that can't be taught but felt.
No one has ever loved me the way you did.
No one will ever love me the way you did.
One momma...you only get one momma.

I'll cherish you forever, and the kids will cherish me, and
then their kids will cherish us until we all meet again,
and again, and again.

I was strong with her,
and now that she's gone,
I'm even stronger because
now I have her strength.

My eyes began to sprinkle. I couldn't hold the storm. The flood of
tears raced down my face when I knew the moment that I dreaded
my entire life had become my new reality. My heart shut off. My
body went still. What would become of my life moving forward?
How would I function the next second I took a breath?
I was shaken.

From that moment on, the person I knew
no longer existed. I didn't
even get to say goodbye to my old self. That's how fast it went.
That's how fast she went. Her last moment was quick, but her life
was long-lived— for her.

It's too late for
regrets now. Don't even start.
You did the best you could with what you knew. And still, till this
day, I am shaken.

There are no endings,
Only new beginnings.
From this world
To the next,
The connection stays.
It grows into a flower,
And that flower
Blooms so bright,
Just like your light—
Always watching over me,
Always guiding me,
Always popping up in my dreams,
In my numbers,
In my sight.
You are there inside of me, watching.

-September 5th

I'll choose better for myself
so that you see
that I know you are always
protecting me.

I'm the seed you planted
Yet I took you for granted
sometimes.
When my time was my time
and I kept you on hold only for the right time.
Just like life, it escapes us, but we must adjust
before moments become memories.
The inevitable is upon us.
So, will you please forgive me?

I wish I did more, I wish I knew better.
So, I write you this letter and send it to a higher power.
I feel your energy, always surrounding me.
Every day and in my sleep.
You passed away on the new moon,
I knew the time would come,
but it was still too soon.

Eleven, seven, twenty eighteen.
Until we meet again, my beautiful queen.
I'll love you forever and ever, Mommy.

-November 7, 2018

heal

Bless the souls who still have yet to feel the pain
and grief from a parent's last goodbyes.

Bless those who will cherish those moments that will one day be
no more.

Bless those who are able to see and appreciate what they have
more than what they want because they have everything.

The rain is over. We're blooming now.

Thank you, Mommy!

.

About the Author

Candace Cotton grew up in Dayton, Ohio, and is a graduate of The Ohio State University. She is the CEO and creator of Candi Naturals Bath and Body Bakery and the author of the children's book series, Zuri Zee's Magical Birthday Adventures. Today, she resides in Los Angeles where she collaborates with illustrators to create short story blogs for children and creates artisanal candles and holistic herbal teas that include inspirational affirmations.

About the Book

Loving myself
is how I healed the pain
from others
who didn't love me.

Just like many of us, Candace Cotton is no stranger to pain and sorrow in her life. In a poignant compilation of mantras, poems, and reflections, Cotton lyrically explores the experiences of trauma and lost love to find hope, healing, and meaning.

Though Cotton is candid about the depth of the heartache that inspired her writings, her collection also brims with resilience and hope that will both uplift and inspire others in their own journeys. While leading others on a path inward to heal from a variety of traumatic experiences, Cotton offers gentle guidance on how to articulate and express difficult emotions and process them with compassion while incorporating self-care into every day.

Heal shares inspiring wisdom and philosophies through poems, mantras, and reflections that address pain, whether small or great, and encourage a journey of learning, healing, and survival.